That Our Faith May Be Tested

A Compilation of Writings

Byrdie Annette Larkin

WESTBOW
PRESS
A DIVISION OF THOMAS NELSON
& ZONDERVAN

WestBow Press books may be ordered through booksellers or by contacting:

WestBow Press
A Division of Thomas Nelson & Zondervan
1663 Liberty Drive
Bloomington, IN 47403
www.westbowpress.com
1 (866) 928-1240

ISBN: 978-1-4908-5546-2 (sc)
ISBN: 978-1-4908-5545-5 (e)

Library of Congress Control Number: 2014917864

Printed in the United States of America.

WestBow Press rev. date: 01/14/2015

Contents

Section III - Life is Love

That our Faith may be Tested

Since childhood I have often written poetry and other creative writings. Why? Perhaps it was my way of adapting to an adult world that I had not yet come to grips with, or perhaps it was a means of creative, spiritual and emotional progression. Many of the writings from my youth were not appreciated enough by me to preserve. And perhaps those are the ones that I would enjoy revisiting today. However, most of the writings appearing in this compilation occurred at the oddest of times – i.e. while I was trying to sleep; while teaching; while relaxing or even when talking to others.

For me, they express an evolution through this world which means that life is a series of experiences. Our lives will be productive and fruitful if we learn from those experiences. I also think that as our Faith in Jesus is tested, we grow spiritually, emotionally and sometimes creatively. The first poem, Why Me, Lord, seemingly sets the stage for the rest of this compilation.

Byrdie A. Larkin

Why Me Lord

Why am I
  in the midst of controversy
Had I not tried
  to avoid getting involved
Why me, Lord

Why am I
  in the midst of exposing injustice
Do I not have enough
  problems to deal with
Why me, Lord

Why am I
  in the midst of this storm
Did I not chart
  my life's goals more carefully
Why me Lord

Why not you
  was the Lord's insightful response

Did I not lead you
     and guide you
     through every controversy
     through every injustice
     through every storm

Did I not bless you
     in the midst of every controversy
     in the midst of every injustice
     in the midst of every storm

And in the midst of
     My <u>own</u> controversies, injustices and storms

Did I not die
     a humiliating and painful death
     for you at Calvary

Then Why Not You?

Dedication with Acknowledgements

<u>That our Faith may be Tested</u> is dedicated to the memories of my mother, Mrs. Lula Berry Larkin and my maternal grandmother, Mrs. Elbirdie Felton Berry. It was through their prayers and guidance that I was nurtured in this Christian walk.

    <u>That our Faith may be Tested</u> is also dedicated to the memory of both Mrs. Mabel Poellnitz and Mrs. Willie Mae Marshall, who are not blood relatives, but fulfilled the motherly void left by the deaths of my mother on September 3, 1980 and her mother, my maternal grandmother, on May 5, 1980.

    And to those who now share in life's experiences-- this compilation is also dedicated to my sister, Ms. Lula Darnell Larkin. Throughout the years, I have also shared my poetry with family and friends, especially my prayer warriors at Mount Gillard Missionary Baptist Church in Montgomery, Alabama. I am also indebted to Mrs. Kay L. Brown, the former Administrative Secretary in the Department of History and Political Science at Alabama State University for helping me to format this document.

To God be the Glory for what He has done!

On Life and Dying

I Have a Dream

*This poem was written as a student upon
the death of Dr. Martin Luther King, Jr.
It is dedicated to his memory.*

Tis only a dream I have
a dream that must come true
it applies to men of all creeds
and leaves within them a thrusting sword

It is a beautiful dream
a dream worthy of kings and queens
It is a just dream…
a dream that God would be proud of
I have a dream

The dream I have is one of eloquence and honor
and everlasting blissfulness;
The dream I have is that all men
whether black or white
can live in complete serenity

Oh black man! Oh white man!
make haste and put my dream to work
Let your hearts so unite as if
we were one

Some say
To dream is foolish
but I say to dream is a wise man's duty
and never ceases throughout life

To dream is to live
and to live is to dream
constantly hoping and praying
for peace

Do you have a dream? Is it a dream of Peace?
Is it a dream of Brotherhood?
Is it a dream of love for all men, disregarding race?
If not, it is not a dream but
merely a nightmare;

Come let us dream together
forgetting all previous quarrels
Let us look toward Heaven
and toward a new home with everlasting peace

Yes – I have a dream
A dream dedicated to all of America
Come and share my dream with me
and live in peace forevermore

The Growing Mother

Written for Mother's Day 1977 in honor of my Mother and Grandmother

The joys and toils of Motherhood
are never realized until
you become a mother
and then

You know what it is to diaper
and change to feed and clean
to chase and hug
and worry, wait
and to finally laugh

Now that I know what it is to be
a mother
I'd just like to say
You did a superb job, Mother
Hope I'll be able to equal it

After reading all the books
listening to my friends,
And trying to observe and experiment
with my own child
I think!!!

I'll follow your model, Mother Dear
And just let my child grow
one day at a time

A Thought for the Teacher

Have you thought as you go to your work each day
that you are a potter who molds the clay
of human life?
As a mason lays bricks from ground to steeple
so are you laying foundations in little people
who will soon grow up
The bricks are ideals and the mortar is truth
Are you making them strong in
the days of their youth
on which they may build?
You give of yourself each day that you live
Are you sure that you're
providing the right things to give?
Each hour of your day
A living monument is yours, my friend
It's the boy or girl you are going to send
out into life
As the weakest link determines the chain
A building is as strong as the foundation lain
so it is with man

So of your material, use only the best
mix it with prayers, with zeal, with zest
And the structure will stand!

*I am not exactly sure when this poem was
written. I was either in junior or high school.
Compare this earlier writing with the more recent
writings included in this book. Interestingly, at
the time that this poem was written I did not
plan to be a teacher. However, my mother was
a public school teacher for thirty-eight years.*

But I can't disappoint Mama and Mother Dear

After returning to my Atlanta home in June 1980 I felt a void in my life because of the death of my maternal grandmother on May 6th. With tears in my eyes I remembered her as both a disciplinarian and an altruist. I thanked God for the comfortable livelihood she had amassed, and her legacy of intellect and multi-talents. I was also saddened by the unexpected death of my father in February 1980.

Perhaps a source of my anxiety was due to the continuing bi-weekly commute from Montgomery, Alabama to teach at Alabama State University. The commute was approximately 160 miles one way. And although my mother had retired only a year earlier and was the constant caregiver to my grandmother, my sisters and I regularly relieved her in caring for our grandmother. And of course I was tired from teaching four classes per semester and working on my dissertation.

And in case I had not mentioned, I was married with a four year old son who traveled with me. Therefore, I had a right to be anxious, but was glad when the summer of 1980 came and I could take my son to vacation Bible School. I also sought Biblical guidance for what I was experiencing. One of our discussions in the adult class that I attended focused on faith healing. Many of the women recounted examples of God's intervention. Why then hadn't God answered my prayers to heal my grandmother? In a motherly way these ladies explained that I had pleased God in displaying my faith, but that His will must be done.

On another occasion our discussion focused on God's revelations. In fact, in the aftermath of family members' deaths, much of what I was now experiencing was the reoccurrences of a two year old dream. I was in Troy, Alabama, my hometown. I was approaching a neighbor's house. What am I doing here? Then I saw my son at the neighbor's door. "Mother, please let me get a piece of cake." "Okay, but you must come home with me." In a burst of energy, he returned and fell into a mud puddle that I had not seen before. Grabbing his arms, I fought frantically to pull him from the mud. But the more I pulled, screamed and perspired, the more he sank. Such physical exertion caused me to awaken abruptly.

I immediately called my mother and asked her about the dream. "It's a sign of death, Byrdie." Not wishing to worry her about my grandmother, I quickly tried to nullify its impact. "Don't worry, Mother Dear, it's not Mama." I frantically looked around the Bible school classroom for comfort. Sensing my desperation, one of the ladies suggested that the dream might mean that I was helping someone.

In late July, I was simply delighted that my mother was visiting us in Atlanta. As we discussed possible decorating ideas I thought how blessed I was to have a mother who was known as "Sweetie" because of her pleasant, considerate disposition. I also thought how well she looked for her 65 years of age and what insightfulness she exhibited.

In late August I prepared to return to Montgomery because I still had been unsuccessful in locating a local job although I was willing to make compromises in my career and salary. Suddenly the telephone rang. It was Darnell, my sister. She was crying and screaming "Mother Dear has had a stroke. She is dragging her right side. Byrdie, come quickly. I'm taking her to the hospital in Dothan." "Can I speak to Mother Dear?" "Byrdie, I'm fine. Don't rush. Darnell, stop crying. I've made my peace with God, and I am prepared…."

It seemed forever until my husband got home from work. As we drove down the winding farm roads,

I prayed please Lord, don't let that dream be about my mother. Arriving at the hospital about 1 a.m. I was wobbly kneed as I opened the door to Room 467 to find tubes attached to my mother's nose as they had been attached to my grandmother's.

My mother assured us that she was not in pain as we kept our vigil The next morning the doctor assured me of my mother's recovery. He said that she might be paralyzed on the right side. Remembering God's promise, Ask and it shall be given, I turned from the doctor and smiled confidently. Although I prayed constantly, I desired to pray with my mother. Afterwards, she moved her right leg. Surely this was a confirmation from God that she would be restored. My confidence was reaffirmed as Mother Dear went to therapy on Labor Day.

In the midst of anticipating recovery, my mother would occasionally ask, why Lord, why. I, too had asked the same question and was just as perplexed. And it was very difficult mustering enough energy to entertain four year olds after hours at the hospital. However, God strengthened us so that our mother was never left unattended. This care and concern was also given to Mother Dear by my Grandmother's adopted daughter, Debbie Coskrey.

On Wednesday evening after Labor Day, the wind blew hard, the sky turned dark, and it rained, as Darnell traveled to the hospital. I had just finished bathing the children when the phone rang. It was Darnell, "Byrdie – Mother Dear is having seizures. Go get the neighbor across the street and come quickly." I felt as I had in my journey to Dothan; that I could physically outrun the car.

As I exited the elevator, I heard the announcement Code 4, Room 467. Not realizing what Code 4 meant, all I could utter was, "Oh God! Please!" After an hour of total frustration, the urgency to pray ceased. An indescribable Hurt took its place as the dejected doctor announced, "we're sorry, but we lost Mrs. Larkin."

How could he lose someone that he was so sure he could help! In my disbelief I was convinced that my mother was dead because of medical negligence or maybe she had worked too hard or maybe she and I had rubbed her leg too hard and long the night before. After many nights of not sleeping, and many days of existing just enough to teach my classes and care for my son, I cried to God to help me to accept my mother's death as an act of Love.

And God is doing just that! Although I have been unable to 'totally' accept my mother's death, God has revealed his handiwork in simple everyday experiences which have caused me to realize that His will cannot be subjected to logic or even commonsense explanations.

The best testimony to be given to my family's legacy of painstaking benevolence and virtuousness is to live a comparable life, fertilizing within my child these same qualities. Such goals take a lifetime and unyielding faith in God, and in accomplishing these goals I will not have disappointed my father, mother and grandmother for I will be in their midst.

This story originally appeared in The Troy Messenger, Sunday March 1, 1981, p. 4A.

Mama   Mother Dear

I Talked to my Child Last Night

A developing, growing coarse
voice greeted my ears
As my authoritative hello
was acknowledged reluctantly

As I continued my parental
instructions
I could not help but notice
that I was not only talking
to my child

But to a man that I had
Borne some few years ago

Pride and Joy

Seve M. Leonard

In 1984 my parents got a divorce. I was only nine years old and was the only child. After the divorce my father was not involved in my life. My mother became my sole provider assuming both parental roles as best she could. The relationship between my mother and me over the next ten years after the divorce has been the biggest impact on my life thus far.

As a child I never felt disadvantaged by my parents' divorce. My mother always has and continues to provide the best she possibly can for me. My mother never remarried, so as a child I became the center of her attention. Her marriage was one of the few failures she has ever experienced. So, she cherished me and virtually dedicated her adult life to pleasing me. She described me as her pride and joy. I was a mama's boy in the worst way.

Around the age of fourteen, the situation began to change. I was starting to become a young man, but I cannot say that I honestly understood what manhood was about. I heard stories about my father during my childhood. There were stories about how suave and cool he was. I could also remember that he smoked. I did not realize it, but I began to emulate my father. I took the same path.

I began to rebel against my mother in search of my manhood. I began to skip school, to drink socially, and to be a playboy. And, as I grew, my problems grew as well. In my senior year in high school I skipped over twenty times. At least twice a week I went to school intoxicated. In 1993 I graduated from high school; I also graduated from a social drinker into a severe alcoholic and found myself on my own at the age of seventeen.

I was terrified! How would I live on the part-time job that I had? My mother was scared of me because her pride and joy was out of control. Because of Tough Love, I soon began to realize what being a man was all about. It was not about how many beers I could drink or how many girls I could get. But, it is about something much deeper than that. And, I can see it so clearly now, as though I am a newborn opening my eyes for the very first time. Being a man is all of those things that my mother has instilled in me over the years. To be a man is to be responsible, to know God, and to perform at my best in everything I do.

As painful as the memories are, I do not regret one day of my life. Those years probably saved my life and my relationship with my mother. I continue to apologize to her for all of the pain I put her through. But, nothing will ever erase all of the nights that she sat up worrying about me. The only way that I can give her back her life is to take control of my life. As a parent, my mother dedicated her life to me. And as her son, I will return the favor. I dream of success for myself as well as for my future family. Most of all, I want to be successful for my pride and joy… my mom. I hope that I am and will forever remain her pride and joy.

By – Seve Mwangi Leonard

Seve Mwangi Leonard is the son of Byrdie A. Larkin. He wrote this manuscript as fulfillment of a college class assignment. This article was printed in <u>Lifted Voices</u>, Virginia M. Jones, Editor, Volume 2 Number 2, Spring 1996, a publication in the Humanities Department of Alabama State University, pp. 36-37.

A short excerpt of this article appears in <u>Writing With Class</u>, 4th. ed., Michelle Denise Dacus, Editor, Boston, MA: Pearson Custom Publishing, 2006, p. 18.

The Facts of Life

Saturday was His only Day Off

He worked from sun up
        until sun down

When he worked
        he knew no pain

His family grew up
        all around him

And he loved them all
        just the same

His woman betrayed him
        and he loved her
        just the same

Because he worked
        he knew no pain

And then one Saturday
        the Lord asked him

Who do you love more
            your work or me?

And as he stuttered,
            confused and sullen

The Lord took his pain away
            and made all his days –
            Saturdays

Without requesting the following poem or knowledge that it was being written, Genesis Ruth Asaray Leonard wrote it upon the occasion of her graduation from the Zelia Stephens Early Childhood Center which is located on the campus of Alabama State University. Genesis is the only grandchild of Byrdie A. Larkin.

We've watched each other learn and grow

We've changed from day to day

I know that all the things we've learned

Will help us along the way

By – Genesis Ruth Asaray Leonard
composed May 2009

Genesis on Graduation Day   Genesis Today

Getting out of Myself

I could really concentrate
    on what is
    to be done
If I could stop thinking
    of
    my needs and desires

I could really do some good
    for others
If I could stop thinking
    of
    my needs and desires

I could offer a word of encouragement
    and hope
If I could stop thinking
    of
    my needs and desires

I could really make a difference
        in this old world
If I could stop thinking
        of
        my needs and desires

And So,
        I'll take the
                first step

I'll make a conscious effort
                to
        refrain from concentrating
                on
        my needs and desires

I'll Ask the Lord
        to
                Help me
                        To Get Out of myself

Being What I'll Never Be

S   wants me to be like this

E   thinks that I emphasize it too much

L   feels that I am too serious

F   questions my cavalier actions

AND

L   again chides me for being too serious

O   demands a decision from me at any cost

V   wants an explanation for my decision

E   again thinks that de-emphasis is warranted

AND

At times I'm confused

AND

At other times my confidence is overwhelming

And in the midst of these

polemics

I am convinced that God has planned

what I should be

And all other requests

are

what I may never be

I Did it
Because
It Felt Good

I did it because
It felt good
I did think about it
But I wanted to do it
And so I did it

I did think about those whom
It might hurt
But I did it anyway
I did it because it felt good

I did think about
what I had been taught

And

How the Good Book would challenge
What I had done
But I did it because it felt good

I did think about the consequences
I did think of the years
That my rash actions might affect
But I did it because it felt good

My mouth is quivering
As I view the object of my temptation
Cushioned in the most appropriate
centers of my desires

And I am utterly weak
as I attempt to ignore its appeal

Oh No!
But I have succumbed

My hand quivers
as I reach for it
My eyes bulge
as I behold its lustful texture
My mind no longer functions
as I whet my tongue

And in its fullness
my stomach groans
attesting
That I have consumed
this entire cake

And the only defense
that I have is that
I did it because it felt good!

Minding My Own Business

If I truly mind
    the minor, not major
details of my life

I will have no time
    to mind
    the major details
    of your life

But if I am minding
    the minor and major
    details of our lives

There will certainly be
    mismanagement
of my own major,
    if not minor business

Spring is in the Air

Spring is in the Air
      can't you smell it
      can't you hear it
      can't you taste it
      can't you see it

Spring is in the Air
      not just to smell
      not just to hear
      not just to taste
      not just to see

But

Spring is a time
      to get in touch
      with the inner self

Spring is a time
      to explore the unknown
      as well as the known

For

Spring illuminates God's omnipotence

The Yellow Bloom

Blooms
> of red, orange, white and sometimes purple
> all grace my garden
> fair and bright

But their spiritedness
> soon fades
> into the distant air

But the yellow blooms
> are special
> meeting the sun

And
> casting contentment over all

But the yellow blooms
> are special
> meeting the grayness
> of a dreary day
> signaling that
> this too, is

God's Day

Because the yellow bloom continues in perpetuity

Nothing Ever Comes Easy

Grind, time, bind
    what I desire
    is not
    forthcoming

Why
    I ask
do I vainly labor
disappointed, worried,
    analytical
    and
    crying
while time elapses

But
    I will just have to wait
For
    Nothing worthwhile
ever comes easy

Life is Love

Of Love and Forgiveness

You rendered the ultimate injustice

Your treatment was that of inhumanness

And though

I suffered no physical infractions

Nor was a hair on my head plucked

Your very actions struck

    at the pulse of existence

And it is a faint

    heart that flutters

year by years

    in the midst of

the hurt and injustices

    that penetrated like a sword

    to the naked flesh

Until one day

      there was no pain

      just awe

And later

      when asked

      to forgive…

Love, unnoticeably

      had already

      intervened

And

      Forgiveness

         taken place

You Taught Me How

Bitter, distrustful and skeptical
    I decided to love again

For years, I remained
    disillusioned, disappointed and unrelenting

Always consumed with work
Always consumed with family
Always consumed with friends
But never maintaining intimacy

Inwardly, I remained
    only a fraction of what
    God had envisioned

But outwardly, I reflected
    achievement
    a sense of beauty
    a delightful charm

Oftentimes, inspiring curiosity
    because of my aloofness

And then –

You made me love again –
    Not only in achievement
    Not only in beauty
    Not only in intellect
    Not only in goals
    Not only in family and friends

But in a sense of Oneness

For in our distinctiveness
    We are one

Because
    Once Again
You taught me how to
    smile confidently
    trust in others
    deal with the superficialities of life

For Once Again
    I am what God envisioned
        in His
        Creation of Adam and Eve

Companions as Friends

We met in a friendly mood

only to be interrupted

We talked, smiled and danced

Only to be interrupted

But when the interruptions
and our actions
Were understood

We talked, smiled, danced and prayed

As our friendship erupted!

And companions became friends

This Beautiful Black Woman

This beautiful black woman
    is crude in her language
    and to some
    crude in her style

This beautiful black woman is not educated
    She is not, to some cultured
    With unbowed head
    For some, she is stereotypical

This beautiful black woman has never
    traveled ten miles
    from her humble home

She is now without mate
    for he preferred more worldly, stately women
Her children now labor with their children
    and some are ashamed
    of her misperceived coarseness

But this beautiful black woman
        Never
Now lets her disappointments
disillusion her

With her full lips, bold and somewhat
        purple from her many years
        of toil and strife

She continues to labor
        without the inspiration of a caring mate
        without the motherly concern from her children
        without sufficient income for today
        to think nothing of tomorrow

But her portrait unveils
        a bent frame where hips
        and breasts once graced

But her portrait unveils
    wrinkled hands
    adorning a wrinkled,
somewhat indistinguishable face

But her portrait unveils
    a woman unscarred by the years
    and the circumstances of her disappointments

This beautiful black woman
    is your mother, grandmother, great-grandmother
    her mother, her mother's mother
    and her mother's mother

This beautiful black woman is you!

Things Fall Apart
Things Come Together

Everything is in disarray
    all at once

Everything needs fixing
    all at once

Everybody needs support
    all at once

    And

Where are my priorities?

But just as surely as
    Things tend to fall apart
When they have seemingly
    disintegrated
    as far as they can

Everything in disarray
        forms wholesomely

Everything that needs fixing
        is adaptable

Everybody needing support
        rekindles spirituality, energies
        and desires

And once Again
Priorities are definable

As Things Come Together

A New Day

Last evening
    it was dark

And
    I could not see
    Where I was going

But
    At twilight
    God spoke

And

    At the break of Dawn

As This New day Began

My Heart and My Mind
    were at Peace

I Looked For Strength

I looked for strength within
    myself

I looked for strength within
    my mother

I looked for strength within
    my father

I looked for strength within
    my sisters and brothers

I looked for strength
    within my mate

And then, I looked for strength within
    other family members

Later, I looked for strength within
    my friends

And when their strength was non-sustaining

And defeat was seemingly

    I found

Strength in God Almighty

Backing into The Door

It was not by forethought
    or even in retrospect

It was not by intelligence
    or even mother wit

It was not the result of prior experiences
    or even future expectations

That I unassumingly
    Thought that I had

Backed into the door
    of success

When in fact it had been God

    Who straightened my back

    Wiped the frown from my face

Turned me straight forwardly around
    From backing into the door

And sent me Forward
     into a world of possibilities

This poem was awarded an Editor's Choice Award and was featured in <u>Collected Whispers</u> by the International Library of Poetry

Not the Time nor the Place

Scurrying, worrying, forgetting

I cannot think

    Because

There is so much

    to do

And so,

    with my back against

        The wall

It is God

    Who brings me

to my senses

    to realize that

its never the time

    nor the place

    to be

scurrying, worrying and forgetting

Lord Not a Lot
But Just Enough

Another unexpected bill
    to accompany
    the many
    that I receive routinely

Another indebtedness
    to accompany
    those that I receive routinely

But the routine ones
    seem to be escalating
    too, too much

And my bank accounts
    seem to have
    a life
    of their own

And by the end
    of the month
    they need life supports

And Lord,
        I think
        Right Now
        I'd like
        not to worry
        anymore
        about money

But retrospectively

        Lord, I realize
                that
        I'd be a better person
                if
        I had just enough
                to make me
                Grateful
        And just enough
        to keep me forever
                Humble

The Long Arm of God

*Dedicated to the memory of the Enterprise
(Alabama) High School students and to ALL
who have lost their lives tragically or in natural
disasters as these students did on March 1, 2007.*

I am sorry that I cannot reach out to you

I am sorry that I cannot send anyone to help you

I am sorry that I am so distressed in
this moment of anxiousness

And so I find that all I can do in desperation

Is to send the Lord Jesus in my stead

For it is He who is the Long Arm of God
and can meet all of our needs

Why Me Lord

Why am I
    in the midst of controversy
Had I not tried
    to avoid getting involved
Why me, Lord

Why am I
    in the midst of exposing injustice
Do I not have enough
    problems to deal with
Why me, Lord

Why am I
    in the midst of this storm
Did I not chart
    my life's goals more carefully
Why me Lord

Why not you
    was the Lord's insightful response

Did I not lead you
    and guide you
    through every controversy
    through every injustice
    through every storm

Did I not bless you
    in the midst of every controversy
    in the midst of every injustice
    in the midst of every storm

And in the midst of
    My <u>own</u> controversies, injustices and storms

Did I not die
    a humiliating and painful death
    for you at Calvary

Then Why Not You?

About the Author

Dr. Byrdie A. Larkin is the daughter of Reverend Charles Haile Larkin and Mrs. Lula Berry Larkin. She was born at John Andrews Hospital in Tuskegee Institute, Alabama; but grew up in Troy, Alabama. Her maternal Grandmother, Mrs. Elbirdie Felton Berry, also played an influential role in her life. She was Valedictorian of her high school graduating class and received a four year scholarship from Alabama State University.

At Alabama State she was a member of Alpha Kappa Mu National Honor Society, the Social Sciences Honor Society and Beta Pi Chapter of Alpha Kappa Alpha Sorority. Graduating Magna Cum Laude from Alabama State University, she received fellowships and scholarships from Notre Dame, Ohio State and Clark Atlanta Universities. She attended Clark Atlanta where she received the Masters of Arts and Doctor of Philosophy degrees in Political Science.

Dr. Larkin is currently the Coordinator and a Professor of Political Science at Alabama State University. She has served as a political analyst for local, state and national media. She has also been interviewed by the British Broadcasting Company. She has organized and served as a panelist on several Voting Rights programs. She is presently a member of the Executive Board of the Alabama Political Science Association where she has also served as President. She is also a member of the National Conference of Black Political Scientists where she has served on its Executive Board and has chaired the committee for Best Paper Award. She is also a member of Pi Sigma Alpha National Political Science Honor Society where she serves as advisor to the Alabama State University chapter. She hopes to begin research on Women Leadership and Activism at Historically Black Colleges and Universities. She has been a Fulbright and Oxford Scholar. One of her most recent listings is in the <u>2000 Outstanding Intellectuals of the 21st Century</u>.

She is the mother of one son, Seve Mwangi Leonard, and the grandmother of Genesis Ruth Asaray Leonard. She has one sister, Ms. Lula Darnell Larkin, and one brother, Mr. Charles H. Larkin, Jr. However, one of her most important achievements is that she is a child of God and a member of the Mount Gillard Missionary Baptist Church where she serves on the Trustee Ministry

Byrdie and Seve